100 Conversations You Need to Have

Volume III • A Chinese Philosophy Guide for Daily Growth

Cherry
Orchard
Books

100 Conversations You Need to Have

Volume III

A Chinese Philosophy Guide for Daily Growth

Perry Giuseppe Rizopoulos

Boston • 2018

Published by Cherry Orchard Books, an imprint of Academic Studies Press.

ISBN 9781618117991 (paperback)

Cover design by Ivan Grave, book design by Tatiana Vernikov.

Academic Studies Press
28 Montfern Avenue
Brighton, MA 02135, USA
press@academicstudiespress.com
www.academicstudiespress.com

For my mother, Dr. Lisa Anne Vacca-Rizopoulos,
Dr. Alfred DiLascia, Dr. Rentaro Hashimoto,
Dr. David Bollert, Dr. Hope Leichter,
Dr. Maxine Greene, and my students,

thank you for opening my eyes to the art of teaching and living.

INTRODUCTION

Philosophy can be the way to a happier and more fulfilling life. It is for everyone and can improve everything you do. The purpose of this journal is to get you started on your journey toward living a more thoughtful and empowered life.

A Brief Statement

Give philosophy your attention and it will fill your mind with questions, your soul with strength, and your body with energy.

—Perry Giuseppe Rizopoulos

The following journal asks many of life's important questions. Write your immediate reaction to each question and then turn the page for further inspiration from some of history's greatest philosophers and write your feelings, interpretations, reflections, and questions about their ideas.

Take a few minutes to write about how your thoughts and the philosopher's ideas can lead you to take action and create. Use these questions and quotes to get to know yourself, to learn how to care for yourself and aim to embody these conversations. Pick this book up, engage with it, put it down and return to it to document and encourage your growth.

That is all you need to do to make this book work for you.

...become simple.

—Marcus Aurelius

1. Why are you reading this book?

Your Answer:

Philosophy's Response:

> Where a target is hung up, arrows will find their way to it.
>
> —Hsün Tzu

Your Comments:

2. How do you challenge yourself?

Your Answer:

Philosophy's Response:

> If you do not climb a high mountain, you will not comprehend the height of the heavens.
>
> —Hsün Tzu

Your Comments:

3. How have you changed this past year? How will you change over this next year?

Your Answer:

Philosophy's Response:

> There is no greater godliness than to transform yourself...
>
> —Hsün Tzu

Your Comments:

4. What skills were you born with?

Your Answer:

Philosophy's Response:

> The gentleman is by birth no different from any other man, it is just that he is good at making use of things.
>
> —Hsün Tzu

Your Comments:

5. What are you lazy about?

Your Answer:

Philosophy's Response:

> When a man is careless and lazy and forgets himself, that is when disaster occurs.
>
> —Hsün Tzu

Your Comments:

6. How do you speak?

Your Answer:

Philosophy's Response:

There are words that invite disaster.

—Hsün Tzu

Your Comments:

7. What goal intimidates you?

Your Answer:

Philosophy's Response:

Great results can be achieved with small forces.

—Sun Tzu

Your Comments:

8. How did you move towards your life's vision today?

Your Answer:

Philosophy's Response:

> Pile up good deeds to create virtue. [. . .] Unless you pile up tiny streams, you can never make a river or a sea.
>
> —Hsün Tzu

Your Comments:

9. When was the last time you quit?

Your Answer:

Philosophy's Response:

Achievement consists in never giving up.

—Hsün Tzu

Your Comments:

10. Do you multitask?

Your Answer:

Philosophy's Response:

He who travels two roads at once will arrive nowhere.

—Hsün Tzu

Your Comments:

11. How do you express your determination?

Your Answer:

Philosophy's Response:

> If there is no dull and determined effort, there will be no brilliant achievement.
>
> —Hsün Tzu

Your Comments:

12. Are you impatient with your goals?

Your Answer:

Philosophy's Response:

If you truly pile up effort over a long period of time, you will enter in the highest realm.

—Hsün Tzu

Your Comments:

13. Who are your mentors?

Your Answer:

Philosophy's Response:

I say that in learning nothing is more profitable than to associate with those who are learned, and of the roads to learning, none is quicker than to love such people.

—Hsün Tzu

Your Comments:

14. How often do you ask for constructive criticism?

Your Answer:

Philosophy's Response:

> He who comes to you with censure is your teacher, he who comes with approbation is your friend; but he who flatters you is your enemy.
>
> —Hsün Tzu

Your Comments:

15. When do you act against your own judgment?

Your Answer:

Philosophy's Response:

> To treat right as right and wrong as wrong is called wisdom; to treat right as wrong and wrong as right is called stupidity.
>
> —Hsün Tzu

Your Comments:

16. How do you plan?

Your Answer:

Philosophy's Response:

He whose actions are few and well-principled is called orderly; he whose actions are many and disorderly is called chaotic.

—Hsün Tzu

Your Comments:

17. How often do you buy new things?

Your Answer:

Philosophy's Response:

> The gentleman uses things; the petty man is used by things.
>
> —Hsün Tzu

Your Comments:

18. How do you view exercise?

Your Answer:

Philosophy's Response:

> Though it may mean labor for the body, if the mind finds peace in it, do it.
>
> —Hsün Tzu

Your Comments:

19. How do you perform at work?

Your Answer:

Philosophy's Response:

If you are shiftless and evasive when it comes to hard work but keen and unrestrained in the pursuit of pleasure, if you are dishonest and insincere, concerned only with your own desires, and inattentive to your work, then you may travel all over the world and though you penetrate to every corner of it, there will be no one who does not reject you.

—Hsün Tzu

Your Comments:

20. Where are you heading in life?

Your Answer:

Philosophy's Response:

If, however, you set a limit to your journey, then you may arrive there sooner or later, before others or after them, but how can you fail to arrive at your goal sometime?

—Hsün Tzu

Your Comments:

21. How do you view small tasks?

Your Answer:

Philosophy's Response:

> Though the road is short, if you do not step along you will never get to the end; though the task is small, if you do not work at it you will never get it finished.
>
> —Hsün Tzu

Your Comments:

22. When do you take breaks?

Your Answer:

Philosophy's Response:

He who takes many holidays will never excel others by very much.

—Hsün Tzu

Your Comments:

23. When and how do you ask for advice?

Your Answer:

Philosophy's Response:

> To deny guide and law and attempt to do everything your own way is to be like a blind man trying to distinguish colors or a deaf man, tones.
>
> —Hsün Tzu

Your Comments:

24. When and where do you feel powerful?

Your Answer:

Philosophy's Response:

Though poor and hard pressed, a gentleman will be broad of will. Though rich and eminent, he will be respectful in his manner.

—Hsün Tzu

Your Comments:

25. What was the last sacrifice you made for someone else?

Your Answer:

Philosophy's Response:

> ...a gentleman must be able to suppress personal desire in favor of public right.
>
> —Hsün Tzu

Your Comments:

26. What are you overdoing?

Your Answer:

Philosophy's Response:

Pride and excess bring disaster.

—Hsün Tzu

Your Comments:

27. What are you responsible for? What are you not responsible for?

Your Answer:

Philosophy's Response:

> The seasons will visit you as they do a well-ordered age, but you will suffer misfortunes that a well-ordered age does not know. Yet you must not curse heaven, for it is merely the natural result of your own actions.
>
> —Hsün Tzu

Your Comments:

28. What are things that you feel good about not doing?

Your Answer:

Philosophy's Response:

> Hence the really skilled man has things which he does not do; the really wise man has things that he does not ponder.
>
> —Hsün Tzu

Your Comments:

29. What can you control?

Your Answer:

Philosophy's Response:

> Therefore, the gentleman cherishes what is within his power and does not long for what is within the power of heaven alone. The petty man, however, puts aside what is within his own power and longs for what is in the power of heaven.
>
> —Hsün Tzu

Your Comments:

30. How did you become a better person this week?

Your Answer:

Philosophy's Response:

> Man's nature is naturally evil; goodness is the result of conscious activity.
>
> —Hsün Tzu

Your Comments:

31. What is something beautiful you saw today?

Your Answer:

Philosophy's Response:

Everything has its beauty but not everyone sees it.

—Confucius

Your Comments:

32. What are you grateful for?

Your Answer:

Philosophy's Response:

> It is better to light one small candle of gratitude than to curse the darkness.
>
> —Confucius

Your Comments:

33. Are you a perfectionist?

Your Answer:

Philosophy's Response:

Better a diamond with a flaw than a pebble without.

—Confucius

Your Comments:

34. Are you angry with anyone right now?

Your Answer:

Philosophy's Response:

When anger rises, think of the consequences.

—Confucius

Your Comments:

35. What are you fully committed to doing?

Your Answer:

Philosophy's Response:

> *Our greatest victory is not in never falling, but in rising every time we fall.*
>
> —Confucius

Your Comments:

36. How do you express love?

Your Answer:

Philosophy's Response:

Loving a thing means wanting it to live.

—Confucius

Your Comments:

37. Are your words bigger than your actions?

Your Answer:

Philosophy's Response:

> A superior man is modest in his speech but exceeds in his actions.
>
> —Confucius

Your Comments:

38. What happens when you do not reach a goal?

Your Answer:

Philosophy's Response:

> When it is obvious that the goals cannot be reached, don't adjust the goals, adjust the action steps.
>
> —Confucius

Your Comments:

39. When and why do you try your best?

Your Answer:

Philosophy's Response:

> Wherever you go, go with all your heart.
>
> —Confucius

Your Comments:

40. When do you feel disrespected?

Your Answer:

Philosophy's Response:

Respect yourself and others will respect you.

—Confucius

Your Comments:

41. What are three things you are taking time to practice today?

Your Answer:

Philosophy's Response:

> To learn something and at times to practice it- surely that is a pleasure.
>
> —Confucius

Your Comments:

42. How do you lead others?

Your Answer:

Philosophy's Response:

> If you keep order among them [those you lead] by means of punishments, the people are without conscience in evading them. If you lead by means of virtue and keep order among them by means of ritual, they have a conscience.
>
> —Confucius

Your Comments:

43. What about life do you confidently understand? What do you confidently not understand?

Your Answer:

Philosophy's Response:

> When you understand something, to recognize that you understand it; but when you do not understand something, to recognize that you do not understand it—that is understanding!
>
> —Confucius

Your Comments:

44. How do you test your beliefs?

Your Answer:

Philosophy's Response:

> He [the gentleman] puts his sayings into action before adopting them as guidelines.
>
> —Confucius

Your Comments:

45. How do you help those who may know less than you?

Your Answer:

Philosophy's Response:

If you promote the good and instruct those who may lack ability they will be encouraged.

—Confucius

Your Comments:

46. How often do you avoid doing what you know is the right thing?

Your Answer:

Philosophy's Response:

> ...to see what is right and not do it is cowardice.
>
> —Confucius

Your Comments:

47. What did you learn from your last mistake?

Your Answer:

Philosophy's Response:

> People's mistakes all come in the same category in that, if one contemplates a mistake, then one gains an understanding of humanness.
>
> —Confucius

Your Comments:

48. What is your reputation?

Your Answer:

Philosophy's Response:

...become fit to be known.

—Confucius

Your Comments:

49. Where does earning money fall in your list of priorities?

Your Answer:

Philosophy's Response:

> The gentleman is familiar with what is right, just as the small man is familiar with profit.
>
> —Confucius

Your Comments:

50. When do you feel insecure around others?

Your Answer:

Philosophy's Response:

When you come across a more skilled person, think of being equal to him. When you come across a less skilled person, turn inwards and examine yourself.

—Confucius

Your Comments:

51. How do you take care of your family?

Your Answer:

Philosophy's Response:

> In serving father and mother, one argues gently. If one sees that they are intent on not following advice, one continues to be respectful and does not show disobedience, and even if one finds it burdensome, one does not feel resentful.
>
> —Confucius

Your Comments:

52. In what ways are you disciplined?

Your Answer:

Philosophy's Response:

> There are few indeed who fail in something through exercising restraint.
>
> —Confucius

Your Comments:

53. What is difficult for you?

Your Answer:

Philosophy's Response:

> The humane man puts difficulties first and success in overcoming them second.
>
> —Confucius

Your Comments:

54. Is your life balanced?

Your Answer:

Philosophy's Response:

> Supreme indeed is the Mean, as a virtue, but for a long time, it has been rare among the people.
>
> —Confucius

Your Comments:

55. What makes you happy?

Your Answer:

Philosophy's Response:

> Even in the midst of eating coarse rice and drinking water and using a bent arm for a pillow happiness is surely to be found; riches and honors acquired by unrighteous means are to me like the floating clouds.
>
> —Confucius

Your Comments:

56. What books have you read this month?

Your Answer:

Philosophy's Response:

> I am not one who knew about things at birth; I am one who through my admiration of antiquity is keen to discover things.
>
> —Confucius

Your Comments:

57. What traits do you admire in your closest friends? Which do you not admire?

Your Answer:

Philosophy's Response:

> When I walk with two others, I always receive instruction from them. I select their good qualities and copy them, and improve on their bad qualities.
>
> —Confucius

Your Comments:

58. When do you become overly emotional?

Your Answer:

Philosophy's Response:

> The gentleman is calm and peaceful; the small man is always emotional.
>
> —*Confucius*

Your Comments:

59. What should you pursue?

Your Answer:

Philosophy's Response:

> The people may be made to follow something, but may not be made to understand it.
>
> —Confucius

Your Comments:

60. How do you express kindness?

Your Answer:

Philosophy's Response:

> Even if one had great talents, supposing one were also arrogant and mean, the rest of one's qualities would simply not be worthy of notice.
>
> —Confucius

Your Comments:

61. What are some flaws in your character?

Your Answer:

Philosophy's Response:

> The Master cut out four things. He never took anything for granted, he never insisted on certainty, he was never inflexible and never egotistical.
>
> —Confucius

Your Comments:

62. What happens when your expectations are not met?

Your Answer:

Philosophy's Response:

There are times, aren't there, when plants shoot but do not flower, and when they flower but do not produce fruit?

—Confucius

Your Comments:

63. What are three words to describe your closest friends?

Your Answer:

Philosophy's Response:

Regard loyalty and good faith as your main concern. Do not make friends of those who are not up to your own standard. If you commit a fault, do not shrink from correcting it.

—Confucius

Your Comments:

64. What worries you? What scares you? What confuses you?

Your Answer:

Philosophy's Response:

> The wise are not perplexed, the humane do not worry, and the courageous do not feel fear.
>
> —Confucius

Your Comments:

65. How do you live by your own advice? How do you advise others?

Your Answer:

Philosophy's Response:

> If one cannot rectify one's own character, what has one to do with rectifying others.
>
> —Confucius

Your Comments:

66. When are you careless?

Your Answer:

Philosophy's Response:

If you are impatient, you will not be thorough.

—Confucius

Your Comments:

67. Whose approval do you seek?

Your Answer:

Philosophy's Response:

> It would be better if the good people among his fellow villagers loved him and the bad people among them hated him.
>
> —Confucius

Your Comments:

68. How do you express humility?

Your Answer:

Philosophy's Response:

> **The gentleman is dignified but not arrogant. The small man is arrogant but not dignified.**
>
> —Confucius

Your Comments:

69. How do you encourage the people around you to grow?

Your Answer:

Philosophy's Response:

> If one loves someone, can one avoid making him work hard? If one is loyal to someone, can one avoid instructing him?
>
> —Confucius

Your Comments:

70. How can you be better at meeting expectations with your family, friends and at work?

Your Answer:

Philosophy's Response:

When one is immodest in speaking about something, carrying it out is difficult.

—Confucius

Your Comments:

71. What are three of your biggest aspirations?

Your Answer:

Philosophy's Response:

> The gentleman reaches out for what is above, the small mean reaches out for what is below.
>
> —Confucius

Your Comments:

72. Who do you rely on for what is important to you?

Your Answer:

Philosophy's Response:

> What the gentleman seeks in himself the small man seeks in others.
>
> —*Confucius*

Your Comments:

73. How are you appreciated by others? How do you express appreciation for others?

Your Answer:

Philosophy's Response:

> The gentleman is pained at the lack of ability within himself; he is not pained at the fact that others do not appreciate him.
>
> —Confucius

Your Comments:

74. What are you often wrong about?

Your Answer:

Philosophy's Response:

The gentleman is correct but not inflexible.

—Confucius

Your Comments:

75. How do you plan for challenges?

Your Answer:

Philosophy's Response:

> He who exercises no forethought but makes light of his opponents is sure to be captured by them.
>
> —Sun Tzu

Your Comments:

76. How do you choose your battles in life?

Your Answer:

Philosophy's Response:

> He will win who knows when to fight and when not to fight.
>
> —Sun Tzu

Your Comments:

77. How are you decisive? How are you indecisive?

Your Answer:

Philosophy's Response:

> Energy may be likened to the bending of a crossbow; decision, to the releasing of a trigger.
>
> —Sun Tzu

Your Comments:

78. How do you learn from success?

Your Answer:

Philosophy's Response:

Do not repeat the tactics which have gained you one victory, but let your methods be regulated by the infinite variety of circumstances.

—Sun Tzu

Your Comments:

79. What was the last impulsive decision you made?

Your Answer:

Philosophy's Response:

Ponder and deliberate before you make a move.

—Sun Tzu

Your Comments:

80. How do you respond to other people's negativity or vices?

Your Answer:

Philosophy's Response:

> Do not swallow bait offered by the enemy.
>
> —Sun Tzu

Your Comments:

81. What are ways you should no longer spend your energy, time or focus?

Your Answer:

Philosophy's Response:

> There are roads which must not be followed.
>
> —Sun Tzu

Your Comments:

82. How do you prepare for possible consequences?

Your Answer:

Philosophy's Response:

> Hence in the wise leader's plans, considerations of advantage and disadvantage will be blended together.
>
> —Sun Tzu

Your Comments:

83. What are your most common excuses?

Your Answer:

Philosophy's Response:

> Throw your soldiers into positions whence there is no escape, and they will prefer death to flight.
>
> —Sun Tzu

Your Comments:

84. When do you acknowledge that you are mortal?

Your Answer:

Philosophy's Response:

> If they [soldiers] will face death, there is nothing they may not achieve.
>
> —Sun Tzu

Your Comments:

85. How do you make sure your next move is your best move?

Your Answer:

Philosophy's Response:

> If it is in your advantage, make a forward move; if not, stay where you are.
>
> —Sun Tzu

Your Comments:

86. What questions do you most often ask yourself?

Your Answer:

Philosophy's Response:

> Three times a day, I ask myself: in dealing with others, have I been faithful? Have I been untrue to friends? Do I practice what I preach?
>
> —Confucius

Your Comments:

87. What are your most frequent negative thoughts?

Your Answer:

Philosophy's Response:

Think no evil.

—Confucius

Your Comments:

88. What do you spread on this earth?

Your Answer:

Philosophy's Response:

> A will set on love is free from evil.
>
> —Confucius

Your Comments:

89. When will your next major project be completed?

Your Answer:

Philosophy's Response:

In action, timeliness matters.

—Lao Tzu

Your Comments:

90. What is your most valuable possession?

Your Answer:

Philosophy's Response:

> Your person or your goods, which is worth more?
>
> —Lao Tzu

Your Comments:

91. What do you want?

Your Answer:

Philosophy's Response:

> There is no crime greater than having too many desires.
>
> —Lao Tzu

Your Comments:

92. What should you learn more about?

Your Answer:

Philosophy's Response:

> Not to know yet to think that one knows will lead to difficulty.
>
> —Lao Tzu

Your Comments:

93. How do you talk about yourself to others?

Your Answer:

Philosophy's Response:

The sage loves himself but does not exalt himself.

—Lao Tzu

Your Comments:

94. How do you respond when things get chaotic?

Your Answer:

Philosophy's Response:

In the midst of chaos, there is also opportunity.

—Sun Tzu

Your Comments:

95. When and how do you make things difficult?

Your Answer:

Philosophy's Response:

The greatest victory is that which requires no battle.

—Sun Tzu

Your Comments:

96. What good habit have you started recently?

Your Answer:

Philosophy's Response:

Opportunities multiply as they are seized.

—Sun Tzu

Your Comments:

97. What are three words that describe you?

Your Answer:

Philosophy's Response:

Know yourself and you will win all battles.

—Sun Tzu

Your Comments:

98. What are you most focused on?

Your Answer:

Philosophy's Response:

> If the mind is willing, the flesh could go on and on without many things.
>
> —Sun Tzu

Your Comments:

99. What have you learned from this book?

Your Answer:

Philosophy's Response:

> Learning continues until death and only then does it cease.
>
> —Hsün Tzu

Your Comments:

100. What will you do with what you've learned?

Your Answer:

Philosophy's Response:

> The learning of the gentleman enters his ear, clings to his mind, spreads through his four limbs and manifests itself in his actions.
>
> —Hsün Tzu

Your Comments:

WORKS CITED

Confucius. *The Analects*. Edited by Raymond Dawson. Oxford: Oxford University Press, 2008.

Lao Tzu. *Chinese Classics: Tao Te Ching*. Edited by Dim C. Lau. Harmondsworth, UK: Penguin Books, 1964.

Sun Tzu. *Art of War*. Minneapolis, MN: Filiquarian Publishing, 2012.

Hsün Tzu. *Basic Writings*. Edited by Burton Watson. New York: Columbia University Press, 1997.

100 Conversations You Need to Have

Volume II
A Stoic Philosophy Guide for Daily Growth

Perry Giuseppe Rizopoulos

Boston • 2018

Published by Cherry Orchard Books, an imprint of Academic Studies Press.

ISBN 9781618117991 (paperback)

Cover design by Ivan Grave, book design by Tatiana Vernikov.

Academic Studies Press
28 Montfern Avenue
Brighton, MA 02135, USA
press@academicstudiespress.com
www.academicstudiespress.com

For my mother, Dr. Lisa Anne Vacca-Rizopoulos,
Dr. Alfred DiLascia, Dr. Rentaro Hashimoto,
Dr. David Bollert, Dr. Hope Leichter,
Dr. Maxine Greene, and my students,

thank you for opening my eyes to the art of teaching and living.

INTRODUCTION

Philosophy can be the way to a happier and more fulfilling life. It is for everyone and can improve everything you do. The purpose of this journal is to get you started on your journey toward living a more thoughtful and empowered life.

A Brief Statement

Give philosophy your attention and it will fill your mind with questions, your soul with strength, and your body with energy.

—Perry Giuseppe Rizopoulos

The following journal asks many of life's important questions. Write your immediate reaction to each question and then turn the page for further inspiration from some of history's greatest philosophers and write your feelings, interpretations, reflections, and questions about their ideas.

Take a few minutes to write about how your thoughts and the philosopher's ideas can lead you to take action and create. Use these questions and quotes to get to know yourself, to learn how to care for yourself and aim to embody these conversations. Pick this book up, engage with it, put it down and return to it to document and encourage your growth.

That is all you need to do to make this book work for you.

...become simple.

—Marcus Aurelius

1. Why are you reading this book?

Your Answer:

Philosophy's Response:

> Accordingly, look about you for the opportunity; if you see it, grasp it, and with all your energy and with all your strength devote yourself to this task.
>
> —*Seneca*

Your Comments:

2. What makes you unique?

Your Answer:

Philosophy's Response:

> Nothing, therefore, is more important than that we should not, like sheep, follow the flock that has gone before us, and thus proceed not where we ought, but where the rest are going.
>
> —*Seneca*

Your Comments:

3. How do you impact others?

Your Answer:

Philosophy's Response:

> ...no one can merely go wrong by himself, but he must become both the cause and the advisor of another's wrongdoing.
>
> —Seneca

Your Comments:

4. How are you careless?

Your Answer:

Philosophy's Response:

> ...certain moments are torn from us, that some be gently removed, and that others glide beyond our reach. The most disgraceful kind of loss, however, is that due to carelessness.
>
> —*Seneca*

Your Comments:

5. How often do you think about the past?

Your Answer:

Philosophy's Response:

Whatever years be behind us are in death's hands.

—*Seneca*

Your Comments:

6. What are you putting off for tomorrow?

Your Answer:

Philosophy's Response:

> ...hold every hour in your grasp. Lay hold of today's task, and you will not need to depend so much upon tomorrow's.
>
> —*Seneca*

Your Comments:

7. What is yours?

Your Answer:

Philosophy's Response:

Nothing is ours except time.

—*Seneca*

Your Comments:

8. When do you work hardest?

Your Answer:

Philosophy's Response:

> Nothing is so certain as that the evils of idleness can be shaken off by hard work.
>
> —*Seneca*

Your Comments:

9. What is a good friend?

Your Answer:

Philosophy's Response:

> But if you can consider any man a friend whom you do not trust as you trust yourself, you are mightily mistaken and you do not sufficiently understand what true friendship means.
>
> —*Seneca*

Your Comments:

10. How do you multitask?

Your Answer:

Philosophy's Response:

Who is everywhere is nowhere.

—*Seneca*

Your Comments:

11. Who do you trust? Why?

Your Answer:

Philosophy's Response:

> It is faulty to trust everyone and to trust no one.
>
> —*Seneca*

Your Comments:

12. When do you feel most alive?

Your Answer:

Philosophy's Response:

> Most men ebb and flow in wretchedness between the fear of death and the hardships of life; they are unwilling to live, and yet they do not know how to die.
>
> —*Seneca*

Your Comments:

13. Do you have good luck?

Your Answer:

Philosophy's Response:

> Unblessed is he who thinks himself unblessed.
>
> —*Seneca*

Your Comments:

14. How do you exercise?

Your Answer:

Philosophy's Response:

> Now there are short and simple exercises which tire the body rapidly, and so save our time; and time is something of which we ought to keep strict account. These exercises are running, lifting weights and jumping.
>
> —*Seneca*

Your Comments:

15. How often do you break a mental sweat?

Your Answer:

Philosophy's Response:

> The mind must be exercised both day and night, for it is nourished by moderate labor, and this form of exercise need not be hampered by cold or hot weather or even by old age.
>
> —*Seneca*

Your Comments:

16. What are you grateful for?

Your Answer:

Philosophy's Response:

> The fool's life is empty of gratitude and full of fears; its course lies wholly toward the future.
>
> —*Seneca*

Your Comments:

17. What do you most frequently desire?

Your Answer:

Philosophy's Response:

> ...we are plunged by our blind desires into ventures which will harm us, but certainly will never satisfy us; for if we could be satisfied with anything, we should have been satisfied long ago; nor do we reflect how pleasant it is to demand nothing, how noble it is to be contented and not be dependent upon luck.
>
> —*Seneca*

Your Comments:

18. What are your most important beliefs?

Your Answer:

Philosophy's Response:

Examine yourself.

—*Seneca*

Your Comments:

19. What motivates your work?

Your Answer:

Philosophy's Response:

> Add statues, paintings and whatever any art has devised for luxury, you will only learn from such things to crave still.
>
> —*Seneca*

Your Comments:

20. When do you feel distracted?

Your Answer:

Philosophy's Response:

> When you are traveling on a road, there must be an end, but when astray, your wanderings are limitless.
>
> —*Seneca*

Your Comments:

21. What are the obligations you try to avoid?

Your Answer:

Philosophy's Response:

It is dishonorable to flinch under a burden.

—*Seneca*

Your Comments:

22. How do you deal with challenges?

Your Answer:

Philosophy's Response:

> ...people love the reward of their hardships, but curse the hardships themselves.
>
> —*Seneca*

Your Comments:

23. How do you respond to negative emotions or situations?

Your Answer:

Philosophy's Response:

> ...what is nastier than to fret at the very threshold of pain.
>
> —*Seneca*

Your Comments:

24. Which of your actions are unnecessary?

Your Answer:

Philosophy's Response:

> Do you ask what is the foundation of a sound mind? It is, not to find joy in useless things.
>
> —*Seneca*

Your Comments:

25. What impacts your happiness?

Your Answer:

Philosophy's Response:

> We have reached the heights if we know what it is that we find joy in and if we have not placed our happiness in the control of externals or things not in our control.
>
> —*Seneca*

Your Comments:

26. How did you challenge yourself this week?

Your Answer:

Philosophy's Response:

> Fire is the test of gold; adversity, of strong people.
>
> —*Seneca*

Your Comments:

27. How are you disciplined?

Your Answer:

Philosophy's Response:

> ...pleasure, unless it has been kept within bounds, tends to rush headlong into the abyss of sorrow.
>
> —*Seneca*

Your Comments:

28. What is your purpose?

Your Answer:

Philosophy's Response:

> For men who leap from one purpose to another, or do not even leap but are carried over by a sort of hazard, how can such wavering and unstable persons possess any good that is fixed and lasting?
>
> —Seneca

Your Comments:

29. Who will you be next year?

Your Answer:

Philosophy's Response:

> ...we should decide what we wish, and abide by the decision.
>
> —*Seneca*

Your Comments:

30. How do you take care of your body?
How do you abuse it?

Your Answer:

Philosophy's Response:

> I confess that we all have an inborn affection for our body; I confess that we are entrusted with its guardianship.
>
> —*Seneca*

Your Comments:

31. What emotions are you good at controlling?

Your Answer:

Philosophy's Response:

> Next, we must follow the old adage and avoid three things with special care: hatred, jealousy and scorn.
>
> —*Seneca*

Your Comments:

32. Why did you decide to do all the things you decided to do today?

Your Answer:

Philosophy's Response:

> ...the wise man regards the reason for all his action, but not the results.
>
> —*Seneca*

Your Comments:

33. What is your relationship with money?

Your Answer:

Philosophy's Response:

> He who craves riches feels fear on their account.
>
> —*Seneca*

Your Comments:

34. What purposes does your money serve?

Your Answer:

Philosophy's Response:

While he puzzles over increasing his wealth, he forgets how to use it.

—*Seneca*

Your Comments:

35. What scares you?

Your Answer:

Philosophy's Response:

Temper your fear with hope.

—*Seneca*

Your Comments:

36. When do you lose track of time?

Your Answer:

Philosophy's Response:

When one is busy and absorbed in one's work, the very absorption affords great delight.

—*Seneca*

Your Comments:

37. How do you express loyalty?

Your Answer:

Philosophy's Response:

> He who begins to be your friend because it pays will also cease because it pays.
>
> —*Seneca*

Your Comments:

38. Do you make gains from your pain?

Your Answer:

Philosophy's Response:

> For our powers can never inspire in us implicit faith in ourselves except when many difficulties have confronted us on this side and on that, and have occasionally even come to close quarters with us, it is only in this way that the true spirit can be tested.
>
> —*Seneca*

Your Comments:

39. What are you afraid of?

Your Answer:

Philosophy's Response:

> We suffer more often in imagination than in reality.
>
> —*Seneca*

Your Comments:

40. What bothers you?

Your Answer:

Philosophy's Response:

> ...some things torment us more than they ought; some torment us before they ought; and some torment us when they ought not torment us at all.
>
> —*Seneca*

Your Comments:

41. Are you nervous for tomorrow?

Your Answer:

Philosophy's Response:

> As to what may happen in the future, we will see later on. Today there is nothing wrong...
>
> —*Seneca*

Your Comments:

42. Why do you fear the things you fear?

Your Answer:

Philosophy's Response:

> We do not put to the test those things which cause our fear...
>
> —*Seneca*

Your Comments:

43. How do you handle a lack of clarity?

Your Answer:

Philosophy's Response:

> How often has the unexpected happened! How often has the expected never come to pass!
>
> —*Seneca*

Your Comments:

44. What are you looking forward to?

Your Answer:

Philosophy's Response:

> You will suffer soon enough when it arrives, so look forward meanwhile to better things.
>
> —*Seneca*

Your Comments:

45. What are you waiting to start?

Your Answer:

Philosophy's Response:

The fool, with all his other faults, has this also, he is always getting ready to live.

—*Seneca*

Your Comments:

46. Where do you go to escape?

Your Answer:

Philosophy's Response:

> Are you surprised as if it were novelty, that after such long travel and so many changes of scene you have not been able to shake the gloom and heaviness of your mind? You need a change of soul rather than a change of climate.
>
> —*Seneca*

Your Comments:

47. Where should you be right now?

Your Answer:

Philosophy's Response:

> You must lay aside the burdens of your mind; until you do this, no place will satisfy you.
>
> —*Seneca*

Your Comments:

48. How do you respond to conflict?

Your Answer:

Philosophy's Response:

> I disagree with those who strike out in the midst of the billows and, welcoming a stormy existence, wrestle daily in hardihood of soul with life's problems. The wise man will endure all that, but will not choose it he will prefer to be at peace rather than at war.
>
> —*Seneca*

Your Comments:

49. What are your friends' goals?

Your Answer:

Philosophy's Response:

This is sound practice—to refrain from associating with people with different aims.

—*Seneca*

Your Comments:

50. Who is holding you back?

Your Answer:

Philosophy's Response:

> Much harm is done even by one who holds you back, especially since life is so short; and we make it still shorter by our unsteadiness...
>
> —*Seneca*

Your Comments:

51. How did you improve today?

Your Answer:

Philosophy's Response:

> Try to perfect yourself, if for no other reason, in order that you may learn how to love.
>
> —*Seneca*

Your Comments:

52. What have you accomplished this month?

Your Answer:

Philosophy's Response:

> When you find out whether you have accomplished anything, consider whether you desire the same things today as you desired yesterday.
>
> —*Seneca*

Your Comments:

53. How many pairs of shoes do you own?

Your Answer:

Philosophy's Response:

> There are but few things needed for a happy life.
>
> —Marcus Aurelius

Your Comments:

54. Is your thinking mostly about the past, the future or the present?

Your Answer:

Philosophy's Response:

> And remember that no one lives more than this infinitesimal point of time, the present; the rest of his days are either lived out or hidden from him.
>
> —Marcus Aurelius

Your Comments:

55. How do you organize your day?

Your Answer:

Philosophy's Response:

> Do not act at random. Understand that there is art in living.
>
> —Marcus Aurelius

Your Comments:

56. How do you handle sadness?

Your Answer:

Philosophy's Response:

> ...remember to apply the following principle when chance brings grief "this thing is no misfortune, but the ability to bear it with fortitude is a blessing indeed."
>
> —Marcus Aurelius

Your Comments:

57. Any regrets?

Your Answer:

Philosophy's Response:

> In every action, ask yourself "What is the character of this act? Will I regret it?"
>
> —Marcus Aurelius

Your Comments:

58. How are things not happening for you?

Your Answer:

Philosophy's Response:

> What can happen without change?
>
> —Marcus Aurelius

Your Comments:

59. How do you feel right now?

Your Answer:

Philosophy's Response:

> All you need are these: certainty in the present moment, action for the common good in the present moment, and an attitude of gratitude in the present moment for anything that comes your way.
>
> —Marcus Aurelius

Your Comments:

60. How do you work with others?

Your Answer:

Philosophy's Response:

> For we are all created to work together, as the members of one body.
>
> —Marcus Aurelius

Your Comments:

61. How do you respond to being wrong?

Your Answer:

Philosophy's Response:

> It is our duty to have these two principles of action ever in readiness: one, to do nothing but what is dictated on behalf of the common good by the ruling and legislative faculty; the other, to be prepared to change our ground if there be found someone who can correct an opinion of ours or point the way to a better one.
>
> —Marcus Aurelius

Your Comments:

62. How will you improve this year?

Your Answer:

Philosophy's Response:

> Act not as though the years of your life were ten thousand. [. . .] While life is yours become good, ere it be too late.
>
> —Marcus Aurelius

Your Comments:

63. How do you bear the burden of other people's mistakes?

Your Answer:

Philosophy's Response:

Does a man sin?—He sins for himself.

—Marcus Aurelius

Your Comments:

64. When do you procrastinate?

Your Answer:

Philosophy's Response:

Time is a rushing torrent stream fed by life and its changes.

—Marcus Aurelius

Your Comments:

65. How do you view your future?

Your Answer:

Philosophy's Response:

> Do not be troubled by the future: you will encounter it with the same sword of reason in your hand that now serves you against the present.
>
> —Marcus Aurelius

Your Comments:

66. How do you speak?

Your Answer:

Philosophy's Response:

Be healthy in word.

—Marcus Aurelius

Your Comments:

67. How do you handle loss?

Your Answer:

Philosophy's Response:

Loss is nothing other than change.

—Marcus Aurelius

Your Comments:

68. Why is your life complicated?

Your Answer:

Philosophy's Response:

> The vast majority of our deeds and words are not necessary. Eliminate these and how much toil and trouble will vanish with them!
>
> —Marcus Aurelius

Your Comments:

69. Do you rely on others for happiness?

Your Answer:

Philosophy's Response:

Happiness is not found in the souls of others but our own.

—Marcus Aurelius

Your Comments:

70. For how much of each day are you present?

Your Answer:

Philosophy's Response:

> Everywhere and at all times, it is up to you to rejoice piously at what is occurring at the present moment, to conduct yourself with justice towards the people who are present...
>
> —Marcus Aurelius

Your Comments:

71. How do you impact those around you?

Your Answer:

Philosophy's Response:

> Have I done an act that benefits the community? Then I have received my reward!
>
> —Marcus Aurelius

Your Comments:

72. How do you accept help?

Your Answer:

Philosophy's Response:

Think it no shame to accept help.

—Marcus Aurelius

Your Comments:

73. Do you need a vacation? Why or why not?

Your Answer:

Philosophy's Response:

> Men are continually seeking retreats from themselves, in the country, or by the sea, or among the hills. Yet all this is the sheerest folly, for it is open to you every hour to retreat into yourself.
>
> —Marcus Aurelius

Your Comments:

74. Are you a morning person?

Your Answer:

Philosophy's Response:

> In the morning, when you rise sorely and against your will, summon up this thought: [...] am I to say I was created for the purpose of lying in blankets and keeping myself warm?
>
> —Marcus Aurelius

Your Comments:

75. How do you learn from mistakes?

Your Answer:

Philosophy's Response:

We must not say that every mistake is a foolish one.

—Cicero*

Your Comments:

---

* Although Cicero did not identify himself as a Stoic, he provided very important reflections on Stoic philosophy, hence our inclusion of his contributions in this volume.

76. How do you behave while angry?

Your Answer:

Philosophy's Response:

> But still anger should be far from us, for nothing is able to be done rightly nor judiciously with anger.
>
> —*Cicero*

Your Comments:

77. What inspires you?

Your Answer:

Philosophy's Response:

> But of all motives, none is better adapted to secure influence than love.
>
> —Cicero

Your Comments:

78. How do you help others?

Your Answer:

Philosophy's Response:

> But if nature prescribes (as she does) that every human being must help every other human being, whoever they are, just precisely because they are all human beings, then all people have identical interests.
>
> —*Cicero*

Your Comments:

79. How do you treat other people when you are having a rough time?

Your Answer:

Philosophy's Response:

> *...every person must bear their own misfortunes rather than remedy them by damaging someone else.*
>
> —*Cicero*

Your Comments:

80. What is your main goal this week?

Your Answer:

Philosophy's Response:

> But as long as we wander at random, not following any guide except the shouts and discordant clamors of those who invite us to go in different directions, our short life will be wasted in useless wandering even if we labor both day and night to get understanding.
>
> —*Seneca*

Your Comments:

81. What makes you happy?

Your Answer:

Philosophy's Response:

True happiness is a verb.

—Epictetus

Your Comments:

82. How do you deal with pain?

Your Answer:

Philosophy's Response:

What is pain? A mask. Turn it and examine it.

—Epictetus

Your Comments:

83. What is your morning routine?

Your Answer:

Philosophy's Response:

> First thing in the morning, we should go over in advance what we have to do during the course of the day, and decide on the principles which will guide and inspire our actions.
>
> —Epictetus

Your Comments:

84. What is your nighttime routine?

Your Answer:

Philosophy's Response:

> In the evening, we should examine ourselves again, so as to be aware of the faults we have committed or the progress we have made. We should examine our dreams.
>
> —Epictetus

Your Comments:

85. What do you imagine most frequently?

Your Answer:

Philosophy's Response:

> We are disturbed not by things, but by the principles and notions which we form concerning things.
>
> —Epictetus

Your Comments:

86. When are you disappointed?

Your Answer:

Philosophy's Response:

> Don't demand that things happen as you wish, but wish that they happen as they do happen...
>
> —Epictetus

Your Comments:

87. How do you give pain a purpose?

Your Answer:

Philosophy's Response:

If you are in pain, you will find fortitude.

—Epictetus

Your Comments:

88. Are you superstitious?

Your Answer:

Philosophy's Response:

> But to me all omens are lucky. For whichever of these things happens, it is in my control to derive advantage from it.
>
> —Epictetus

Your Comments:

89. Do you think before you act?

Your Answer:

Philosophy's Response:

> In every affair consider what precedes and follows, and then undertake it.
>
> —Epictetus

Your Comments:

90. Are your actions focused?

Your Answer:

Philosophy's Response:

> ...you too will be at one time a wrestler, at another a gladiator, now a philosopher, then an orator; but with your whole soul, nothing at all.
>
> —Epictetus

Your Comments:

91. Do you change when the people around you change?

Your Answer:

Philosophy's Response:

> Immediately prescribe some character and form of conduct to yourself, which you may keep both alone and in company.
>
> —Epictetus

Your Comments:

92. Who is your most positive friend?

Your Answer:

Philosophy's Response:

> ...if his companion be infected, he who converses with him will likewise be infected.
>
> —Epictetus

Your Comments:

93. Are you always waiting for the weekend to be happy?

Your Answer:

Philosophy's Response:

> Neither should a ship rely on one small anchor nor should life rest on a single hope.
>
> —Epictetus

Your Comments:

94. When was the last time things went very well for you? How and why did this happen?

Your Answer:

Philosophy's Response:

> We should enjoy good fortune while we have it, like the fruits of autumn.
>
> —Epictetus

Your Comments:

95. How do you deal with negative people?

Your Answer:

Philosophy's Response:

> Don't regard what anyone says of you, for this, after all, is no concern of yours.
>
> —Epictetus

Your Comments:

96. Do you compare yourself to others?

Your Answer:

Philosophy's Response:

> Stop aspiring to be anyone other than your own best self: for that does fall within your control.
>
> —Epictetus

Your Comments:

97. Who are your closest friends?

Your Answer:

Philosophy's Response:

> Be careful whom you associate with. We inadvertently adopt their interests, their opinions, their values and their habit of interpreting events.
>
> —Epictetus

Your Comments:

98. What is the greatest version of your future self?

Your Answer:

Philosophy's Response:

> Decide to be extraordinary and do what you need to do, now.
>
> —Epictetus

Your Comments:

99. What have you learned from this book?

Your Answer:

Philosophy's Response:

> Only the educated are free.
>
> —Epictetus

Your Comments:

100. What will you do with what you've learned?

Your Answer:

Philosophy's Response:

> Set yourself in motion, if it is in your power, and do not
> look about you to see if anyone will observe it;
> but be content if the smallest things goes on well,
> and consider such an event to be no small matter.
>
> —Marcus Aurelius

Your Comments:

WORKS CITED

Marcus Aurelius. *Meditations*. Edited by George Long. Seattle, WA: CreateSpace Independent Publishing Platform, 2017.

Cicero, Marcus Tullius. *Cicero: Selected Works*. Edited by Michael Grant. Harmondsworth, UK: Penguin Books, 1965.

Epictetus. *A Selection from the Discourses of Epictetus with the Encheiridion*. Edited by George Long. Whitefish, MT: Kessinger, 2007.

Epictetus. *The Art of Living: the Classic Manual on Virtue, Happiness, and Effectiveness*. Edited by Sharon Lebell. New York: HarperOne, 2007.

Seneca, Lucius Annaeus. *Seneca Six Pack: Six Essential Texts*. Translated by Richard M. Gummere, Ella Isabel Harris, Aubrey Stewart. Los Angeles, CA: Enhanced Media Publishing, 2016.

100 Conversations You Need to Have

Volume I
A Philosophy Guide for Daily Growth

Perry Giuseppe Rizopoulos

Boston • 2018

Published by Cherry Orchard Books, an imprint of Academic Studies Press.

ISBN 9781618117991 (paperback)

Cover design by Ivan Grave, book design by Tatiana Vernikov.

Academic Studies Press
28 Montfern Avenue
Brighton, MA 02135, USA
press@academicstudiespress.com
www.academicstudiespress.com

For my mother, Dr. Lisa Anne Vacca-Rizopoulos,
Dr. Alfred DiLascia, Dr. Rentaro Hashimoto,
Dr. David Bollert, Dr. Hope Leichter,
Dr. Maxine Greene, and my students,

thank you for opening my eyes to the art of teaching and living.

INTRODUCTION

Philosophy can be the way to a happier and more fulfilling life. It is for everyone and can improve everything you do. The purpose of this journal is to get you started on your journey toward living a more thoughtful and empowered life.

A Brief Statement

Give philosophy your attention and it will fill your mind with questions, your soul with strength, and your body with energy.

—Perry Giuseppe Rizopoulos

The following journal asks many of life's important questions. Write your immediate reaction to each question and then turn the page for further inspiration from some of history's greatest philosophers and write your feelings, interpretations, reflections, and questions about their ideas.

Take a few minutes to write about how your thoughts and the philosopher's ideas can lead you to take action and create. Use these questions and quotes to get to know yourself, to learn how to care for yourself and aim to embody these conversations. Pick this book up, engage with it, put it down and return to it to document and encourage your growth.

That is all you need to do to make this book work for you.

...become simple.

—Marcus Aurelius

1. Why are you reading this book?

Your Answer:

Philosophy's Response:

Stick with your purpose. This alone will strengthen your will and give your life coherence.

—Epictetus

Your Comments:

2. How could your life be better?

Your Answer:

Philosophy's Response:

The universe is change, our life is what our thoughts make it.

—Marcus Aurelius

Your Comments:

3. What qualities are you developing?

Your Answer:

Philosophy's Response:

> Never stop sculpting your own statue, until the divine virtue of splendor shines in you.
>
> —Plotinus

Your Comments:

4. How often are you doing "nothing"?

Your Answer:

Philosophy's Response:

...man is constantly in the making.

—Jean-Paul Sartre

Your Comments:

5. How have you taken action today to pursue growth?

Your Answer:

Philosophy's Response:

> ...so those who act, win, and rightly win, the noble and good things in life.
>
> —Aristotle

Your Comments:

6. How do you respond to change?

Your Answer:

Philosophy's Response:

Change is the only constant.

—Heraclitus

Your Comments:

7. In what areas should you be more confident?

Your Answer:

Philosophy's Response:

> Both in feeling and in conduct, habit is the only thing which imparts certainty...
>
> —John Stuart Mill

Your Comments:

8. Is the grass always greener on the other side?

Your Answer:

Philosophy's Response:

> Without giving up hope that there's somewhere better to be, that there's someone better to be—
> we will never relax with where we are and who we are.
>
> —Pema Chödrön

Your Comments:

9. Whose opinion of you matters the most?

Your Answer:

Philosophy's Response:

> I have often marveled how it is that everyone loves themselves more than the rest of human kind, yet values their own opinion of themselves less than that of others.
>
> —Marcus Aurelius

Your Comments:

10. What do you enjoy doing?

Your Answer:

Philosophy's Response:

> A man should not pursue every pleasure, but that pleasure which leads to goodness.
>
> —Epictetus

Your Comments:

11. How do you respond to other people's achievements?

Your Answer:

Philosophy's Response:

There is no misfortune greater than being jealous.

—Lao Tzu

Your Comments:

12. How big do you dream? What is your most ridiculous dream?

Your Answer:

Philosophy's Response:

All great deeds and all great thoughts have a ridiculous beginning.

—Albert Camus

Your Comments:

13. How do you plan?

Your Answer:

Philosophy's Response:

> There always comes a time when one must choose between contemplation and action. This is called becoming.
>
> —Albert Camus

Your Comments:

14. When do you become discouraged?

Your Answer:

Philosophy's Response:

Nothing great is easy.

—Plato

Your Comments:

15. What do you want?

Your Answer:

Philosophy's Response:

> It is thus clear that of all goods, happiness is the greatest. And of all preferred things, happiness is the most perfect end that man has ever desired.
>
> —Al-Fārābi

Your Comments:

16. When do you take time to reflect?

Your Answer:

Philosophy's Response:

> To take flight every day! At least for a moment, which may be brief, as long as it is intense. A "spiritual exercise" every day—either alone, or in the company of someone who also wishes to better themselves.
>
> —Georges Friedmann

Your Comments:

17. What did you learn from your conversations this week?

Your Answer:

Philosophy's Response:

> True education is always oral because only the spoken word makes dialogue possible...
>
> —Pierre Hadot

Your Comments:

18. How do you respond to traffic?

Your Answer:

Philosophy's Response:

> ...if it concerns anything not in your control,
> be prepared to say that it is nothing to you.
>
> —Epictetus

Your Comments:

19. Who will you become this year?

Your Answer:

Philosophy's Response:

Man is nothing other than what he makes of himself.

—Jean-Paul Sartre

Your Comments:

20. How are you impatient?

Your Answer:

Philosophy's Response:

> Remember that you must behave in life as at a dinner party. Is anything brought around you? Put out your hand and take your share with moderation. Does it pass by you? Don't stop it. Is it not yet come? Don't stretch your desire toward it, but wait till it reaches you.
>
> —Epictetus

Your Comments:

21. How are you influenced?

Your Answer:

Philosophy's Response:

> All I maintain is that on this earth there is pestilence and there are victims, and it's up to us, so far as possible, not to join forces with the pestilence.
>
> —Albert Camus

Your Comments:

22. What are your happiness habits?

Your Answer:

Philosophy's Response:

> We can see the role habit plays in what makes someone happy.
>
> —Al-Fārābi

Your Comments:

23. What is the last book you read? What did you learn?

Your Answer:

Philosophy's Response:

Books are the training weights of the mind.

—Epictetus

Your Comments:

24. What are the things you do every day?

Your Answer:

Philosophy's Response:

...virtue comes about as a result of habit.

—Aristotle

Your Comments:

25. How do you procrastinate?

Your Answer:

Philosophy's Response:

> Change your life today. Don't gamble on the future, act now, without delay.
>
> —Simone de Beauvoir

Your Comments:

26. When do you rush?

Your Answer:

Philosophy's Response:

> Your true destination is the here and the now, because only in this moment and in this place is life possible.
>
> —Thich Nhat Hanh

Your Comments:

27. Whose opinion do you consider? Why?

Your Answer:

Philosophy's Response:

> Socrates: "But why, my dear Crito, should we care about the opinion of the many? Good men, they are the only persons who are worth considering..."
>
> —Plato

Your Comments:

28. What tempts you?

Your Answer:

Philosophy's Response:

> It is the part of the wise man to resist pleasure, but of the foolish man to be slave to them.
>
> —Epictetus

Your Comments:

29. How do you solve problems?

Your Answer:

Philosophy's Response:

> ...many gifts are within your reach at any and every moment.
>
> —Marcus Aurelius

Your Comments:

30. How do you create a more just world?

Your Answer:

Philosophy's Response:

> A man running a race in the stadium should try his best and exert himself to the utmost in order to win. In no circumstances, however, should he trip up his competitors or impede them with his hand. Anyone may fairly seek his own advantage, but no one has the right to do so at another's expense.
>
> —*Cicero*

Your Comments:

31. Who do you love?

Your Answer:

Philosophy's Response:

True love gives us beauty, freshness, solidity, freedom, and peace. True love includes a feeling of deep joy that we are alive. If we don't feel this way when we feel love, then it's not true love.

—Thich Nhat Hanh

Your Comments:

32. Do you help others? How do you help others?

Your Answer:

Philosophy's Response:

Help others, life is short.

—Marcus Aurelius

Your Comments:

33. What do you say most often?

Your Answer:

Philosophy's Response:

One should not act and speak like people asleep.

—Marcus Aurelius

Your Comments:

34. How do you respond to insults?

Your Answer:

Philosophy's Response:

> The potential beauty of human life is constantly made ugly by man's ever-recurring song of retaliation.
>
> —Dr. Martin Luther King Jr.

Your Comments:

35. What are you expecting this year?

Your Answer:

Philosophy's Response:

> Wherever you find yourself and in whatever circumstances, give an impeccable performance.
>
> —Epictetus

Your Comments:

36. When was the last time you genuinely smiled?

Your Answer:

Philosophy's Response:

> Man only likes to count his troubles, but he does not count his joys.
>
> —Fyodor Dostoyevsky

Your Comments:

37. What stops you from starting?

Your Answer:

Philosophy's Response:

> Start where you are. You might be the most depressed person, the most addicted person in the world, the most jealous person in the world. You might think that there are no other people on the planet who hate themselves as much as you do. All of that is a good place to start. Just where you are—that's the place to start.
>
> —Pema Chödrön

Your Comments:

38. Are you unhappy right now?

Your Answer:

Philosophy's Response:

> ...the conscious ability to do without happiness gives the best opportunity of realizing that happiness is attainable.
>
> —John Stuart Mill

Your Comments:

39. How are you a good friend?

Your Answer:

Philosophy's Response:

> I am not your friend unless whatever is at issue concerning you is my concern also.
>
> —*Seneca*

Your Comments:

40. Do you make lemonade out of lemons or lemons out of lemonade?

Your Answer:

Philosophy's Response:

> If the descent is thus sometimes performed in sorrow, it can also take place in joy.
>
> —Albert Camus

Your Comments:

41. How would you describe “negative” emotions?

Your Answer:

Philosophy's Response:

> In reality, when you feel depressed, lonely, betrayed or any unwanted feelings, this is an important moment on the spiritual path. This is when real transformation can take place.
>
> —Pema Chödrön

Your Comments:

42. How much time do you spend thinking about time?

Your Answer:

Philosophy's Response:

> Likewise and during every day of an unillustrious life, time carries us. But a moment always comes when we have to carry it.
>
> —Albert Camus

Your Comments:

43. Why do you become upset?

Your Answer:

Philosophy's Response:

> The cure will not be found for any pain whose causes are not known.
>
> —Al-Kindī

Your Comments:

44. How do you care for yourself?

Your Answer:

Philosophy's Response:

> *If we take good care of ourselves, we help everyone.*
>
> —Thich Nhat Hanh

Your Comments:

45. What are you afraid of?

Your Answer:

Philosophy's Response:

> First, we must unflinchingly face our fears and honestly ask ourselves why we are afraid. This confrontation will, to some measure, grant us power.
>
> —Dr. Martin Luther King Jr.

Your Comments:

46. What are some habits you should change?

Your Answer:

Philosophy's Response:

Many indifferent things, which men originally did from a motive of some sort, they continue to do from habit.

—John Stuart Mill

Your Comments:

47. How do you create balance in life?

Your Answer:

Philosophy's Response:

> So much, then is plain that the intermediate state is in all things to be praised, but that we must incline sometimes toward the excess, sometimes toward deficiency; for so shall we most easily hit the mean and what is right.
>
> —Aristotle

Your Comments:

48. How would you define a miracle?

Your Answer:

Philosophy's Response:

> When I breathe in and become fully alive, I see myself as a miracle.
>
> —Thich Nhat Hanh

Your Comments:

49. How have your relationships grown this year?

Your Answer:

Philosophy's Response:

The moment love stops growing, it begins to die.

—Thich Nhat Hanh

Your Comments:

50. How do you plan your day?

Your Answer:

Philosophy's Response:

> If one does not know to which port one is sailing, no wind is favorable.
>
> —*Seneca*

Your Comments:

51. What did you learn today?

Your Answer:

Philosophy's Response:

> ...the source of wisdom is whatever is happening to us right at this very instant.
>
> —Pema Chödrön

Your Comments:

52. Why do you love the people that you love?

Your Answer:

Philosophy's Response:

> At Oran, as elsewhere, for lack of time and thinking, people have to love one another without knowing much about it.*
>
> —Albert Camus

Your Comments:

* Author's note: We might live in Oran but we shouldn't. Don't let your love become numb or meaningless.

53. How do you handle new and unfamiliar tasks?

Your Answer:

Philosophy's Response:

> ...we must begin with things known to us.
>
> —Aristotle

Your Comments:

54. Do you daydream frequently?

Your Answer:

Philosophy's Response:

...reality alone counts...

—Jean-Paul Sartre

Your Comments:

55. How do you strive for your biggest aspirations?

Your Answer:

Philosophy's Response:

> ...it is by forcing the soul into praiseworthy habits in the smallest affairs [...] that one progresses to forcing the soul in greater affairs.
>
> —Al-Kindī

Your Comments:

56. Which of your actions are necessary?

Your Answer:

Philosophy's Response:

> For the vast majority of our deeds and words are not necessary. Eliminate these, and how much toil and trouble will vanish with them!
>
> —Marcus Aurelius

Your Comments:

57. How do you apply what you learn?

Your Answer:

Philosophy's Response:

> ...it is enough to drive one to both laughter and tears to see how all this knowledge and understanding exercises no influence at all on people's lives...
>
> —Søren Kierkegaard

Your Comments:

58. What desires drive you most?

Your Answer:

Philosophy's Response:

> Have little thought of self and as few desires as possible.
>
> —Lao Tzu

Your Comments:

59. What do you think of your friends?

Your Answer:

Philosophy's Response:

> For what purpose, then, do I make a man my friend? In order to have someone for who I may die, whom I may follow into exile, against whose death I may stake my own life, and pay the pledge too.
>
> —*Seneca*

Your Comments:

60. How are you engaging with the questions in this book?

Your Answer:

Philosophy's Response:

Spiritual exercises are required for the healing of the soul.

—Pierre Hadot

Your Comments:

61. Do your words match your actions?

Your Answer:

Philosophy's Response:

> One of the greatest tragedies of life is that men seldom bridge the gulf between practice and profession, between doing and saying.
>
> —Dr. Martin Luther King Jr.

Your Comments:

62. What do you value in your significant other?

Your Answer:

Philosophy's Response:

> When you love someone, you have to respect her, not only her mind but also her body.
>
> —Thich Nhat Hanh

Your Comments:

63. How do you express love?

Your Answer:

Philosophy's Response:

> In reality, however, for the existentialists, there is no love other than the deeds of love; no potential for love other than that which is manifested in loving.
>
> —Jean-Paul Sartre

Your Comments:

64. Are you always true to yourself?

Your Answer:

Philosophy's Response:

> ...what is evil is precisely to be who you are not.
>
> —Al-Kindī

Your Comments:

65. How do you handle failure?

Your Answer:

Philosophy's Response:

> ...letting things fall apart would actually let fresh air into this old, stale basement of a heart that we've got.
>
> —Pema Chödrön

Your Comments:

66. How do you get in your own way?

Your Answer:

Philosophy's Response:

He who overcomes others has force. He who overcomes himself is strong.

—Lao Tzu

Your Comments:

67. What are you passionate about?

Your Answer:

Philosophy's Response:

Beauty will save the world.

—Fyodor Dostoyevsky

Your Comments:

68. When do you make time for learning?

Your Answer:

Philosophy's Response:

Unlike physical blindness that is usually inflicted upon individuals as a result of natural forces beyond their control, intellectual and moral blindness is a dilemma which man inflicts upon himself by his tragic misuse of freedom and his failure to use his mind to its fullest capacity.

—Dr. Martin Luther King Jr.

Your Comments:

69. What "impossible" goal should you work to achieve?

Your Answer:

Philosophy's Response:

> Do not think that what is hard for you to do is humanly impossible, but if a thing is humanly possible, consider it to be within your reach.
>
> —Marcus Aurelius

Your Comments:

70. How often do you escape?

Your Answer:

Philosophy's Response:

> We think that by protecting ourselves from suffering we are being kind to ourselves. The truth is we only become more fearful, more hardened and more alienated.
>
> —Pema Chödrön

Your Comments:

71. How would you describe your behavior?

Your Answer:

Philosophy's Response:

> ...one should always ask oneself, "What would happen if everyone did what I am doing?"
>
> —Jean-Paul Sartre

Your Comments:

72. What is a task you consistently struggle with?

Your Answer:

Philosophy's Response:

> For habit, as the ancient philosophers said, is a second nature that can make what is difficult seem easy [...] whether it be in matters of the soul or the body...
>
> —Ar-Rāzī

Your Comments:

73. How do you express your thoughts?

Your Answer:

Philosophy's Response:

> *...there is no genius other than that which is expressed in works of art.*
>
> —Jean-Paul Sartre

Your Comments:

74. What did you consume this week?

Your Answer:

Philosophy's Response:

> There are four kinds of food that we consume every day. They are edible food (what we put into our mouths to nourish our bodies), sensory food (what we smell, hear, taste, feel and touch), volition (the motivation and intention that fuels us) and consciousness (this includes our individual consciousness, the collective consciousness and our environment).
>
> —Thich Nhat Hanh

Your Comments:

75. How do you feel right now?

Your Answer:

Philosophy's Response:

> We can aspire to be kind right in the moment, to relax and open our heart and mind to what is in front of us right in the moment. Now is the time.
>
> —Pema Chödrön

Your Comments:

76. How do you add value to the world around you?

Your Answer:

Philosophy's Response:

> But practically I know men and recognize them
> by their behavior, by the totality of their deeds,
> by consequences caused in life by their presence.
>
> —Albert Camus

Your Comments:

77. Who are the most important people to you? Why?

Your Answer:

Philosophy's Response:

> One's life has value so long as one attributes value to the life of others, by means of love, friendship, indignation and compassion.
>
> —Simone de Beauvoir

Your Comments:

78. Are you a perfectionist?

Your Answer:

Philosophy's Response:

> Seeking security or perfection, rejoicing in feeling confirmed as whole, self-contained and comfortable, is some kind of death...
>
> —Pema Chödrön

Your Comments:

79. How do you usually make decisions?

Your Answer:

Philosophy's Response:

> If it is not right, do not do it; if it is not true, do not say it.
>
> —Marcus Aurelius

Your Comments:

80. What do you do when you are angry?

Your Answer:

Philosophy's Response:

> If you do not wish to be prone to anger, do not feed the habit; give it nothing which may tend to its increase.
>
> —Epictetus

Your Comments:

81. Why will you get out of bed tomorrow?

Your Answer:

Philosophy's Response:

> Rising, streetcar, four hours of work, meal, sleep, Monday, Tuesday, Wednesday, Thursday, Friday and Saturday according to the same rhythm—this path is easily followed most of the time. But one day the "why" arises and everything begins in that weariness tinted with amazement. "Begins"—this is important, weariness comes at the end of the acts of a mechanical life, but at the same time, it inaugurates the impulse of consciousness.
>
> —Albert Camus

Your Comments:

82. Do you wake up and take a sleeping pill?

Your Answer:

Philosophy's Response:

> Life's work is to wake up, to let the things that enter your life wake you up rather than put you to sleep.
>
> —Pema Chödrön

Your Comments:

83. How do you create a sense of tranquility?

Your Answer:

Philosophy's Response:

> The still is the lord of the restless.
>
> —Lao Tzu

Your Comments:

84. When did you last visit a new place?

Your Answer:

Philosophy's Response:

The sun is new each day.

—Aristotle

Your Comments:

85. What or whom do you believe in?

Your Answer:

Philosophy's Response:

> For our trouble is simply that we attempt to confront fear without faith; we sail through the stormy seas of life without adequate spiritual boats.
>
> —Dr. Martin Luther King Jr.

Your Comments:

86. What are your most important responsibilities?

Your Answer:

Philosophy's Response:

> ...man is responsible for what he is.
>
> —Jean-Paul Sartre

Your Comments:

87. What do you focus on?

Your Answer:

Philosophy's Response:

> Tell me what you pay attention to and I will tell you who you are.
>
> —José Ortega y Gasset

Your Comments:

88. Do you stop to smell the roses?

Your Answer:

Philosophy's Response:

> If, then, I were asked for the most important advice I could give, that which I considered to be the most useful to the men of our century, I should simply say: in the name of God, stop a moment, cease your work, look around you.
>
> —Leo Tolstoy

Your Comments:

89. How did you challenge yourself this week?

Your Answer:

Philosophy's Response:

> The struggle itself toward the heights is enough to fill a man's heart.
>
> —Albert Camus

Your Comments:

90. What are three words that describe you?

Your Answer:

Philosophy's Response:

> Man is nothing other than his own project. He exists only to the extent that he realizes himself, therefore he is nothing more than the sum of his actions, nothing more than his life.
>
> —Jean-Paul Sartre

Your Comments:

91. How do you handle mistakes?

Your Answer:

Philosophy's Response:

> Anyone can make mistakes, but only a fool persists in their error.
>
> —*Cicero*

Your Comments:

92. How are you rich?

Your Answer:

Philosophy's Response:

A good mind possesses a kingdom.

—*Seneca*

Your Comments:

93. What events have been your greatest teachers? What did you learn from them?

Your Answer:

Philosophy's Response:

> We do not learn from experience; we learn from reflecting on experience.
>
> —John Dewey

Your Comments:

94. What will be your next achievement?

Your Answer:

Philosophy's Response:

> ...a blind man eager to see who knows the night has no end, he is still on the go. The rock is still rolling.
>
> —Albert Camus

Your Comments:

95. How do you make those whom you love happy?

Your Answer:

Philosophy's Response:

> If a relationship can't provide joy, then it's not true love. If you keep making the other person cry all day, that's not true love.
>
> —Thich Nhat Hanh

Your Comments:

96. What did you eat today?

Your Answer:

Philosophy's Response:

> If we don't eat healthy foods and don't treat our bodies with respect, then how can we respect other people's bodies and the body of the earth itself?
>
> —Thich Nhat Hanh

Your Comments:

97. What do you do when you succeed?

Your Answer:

Philosophy's Response:

> That which advantages not the hive advantages not the bee.
>
> —Marcus Aurelius

Your Comments:

98. How do you contradict yourself?

Your Answer:

Philosophy's Response:

> On the one hand, we proudly profess certain sublime and noble principles, but on the other hand, we sadly practice the antithesis of those principles.
>
> —Dr. Martin Luther King Jr.

Your Comments:

99. What is stopping you from being the person you want to be?

Your Answer:

Philosophy's Response:

What stands in the way, becomes the way.

—Marcus Aurelius

Your Comments:

100. Do you seek the approval of others?

Your Answer:

Philosophy's Response:

> Never depend on the admiration of others. There is no strength in it. Personal merit cannot be derived from an external source.
>
> —Epictetus

Your Comments:

101. What have you learned from this book?

Your Answer:

Philosophy's Response:

Education is soul crafting.

—Dr. Cornel West

Your Comments:

102. What will you do with what you've learned?

Your Answer:

Philosophy's Response:

> Be strong and of good courage, act for the best, hope for the best and take what comes… if death ends all, we cannot meet death better.
>
> —William James

Your Comments:

SUGGESTED READING

Antoninus, Marcus Aurelius, and John Jackson. *The Thoughts of Marcus Aurelius Antoninus*. London: Oxford University Press, 1962.

Beauvoir, Simone de. *The Second Sex*. New York: Vintage Classic, 2015.

Becker, Ernest. *The Denial of Death*. New York: Free, 1973.

Camus, Albert. *The Stranger*. Edited by G. J. Gillis and Selena Ward. New York: Spark Pub., 2002.

Foucault, Michel. *The Hermeneutics of the Subject: Lectures at the Collège De France, 1981-1982*. Edited by Frédéric Gros, translated by Graham Burchell. London: Picador, 2006.

Gelb, Michael. *How to Think like Leonardo Da Vinci: Seven Steps to Every Day Genius*. London: Thorsons, 1998.

Holiday, Ryan, and Stephen Hanselman. *The Daily Stoic: 366 Meditations on Wisdom, Perseverance, and the Art of Living*. London: Portfolio/Penguin, 2016.

Marino, Gordon Daniel. "The Case for Animal Rights." In *Ethics: The Essential Writings*, edited by Gordon Daniel Marino, 530–544. New York: Modern Library, 2010.

Marino, Gordon Daniel. "The Disparity Between Intellect and Character." In *Ethics: The Essential Writings*, edited by Gordon Daniel Marino, 350–355. New York: Modern Library, 2010. .

Marino, Gordon Daniel. "Euthyphro." In *Ethics: The Essential Writings*, edited by Gordon Daniel Marino, 6–23. New York: Modern Library, 2010.

Marino, Gordon Daniel. "From Cruelty to Goodness." In *Ethics: The Essential Writings*, edited by Gordon Daniel Marino, 333–349. New York: Modern Library, 2010.

Marino, Gordon Daniel. "Letter From a Birmingham Jail." In *Ethics: The Essential Writings*, edited by Gordon Daniel Marino, 356–377. New York: Modern Library, 2010.

Marino, Gordon Daniel. "Rich and Poor." In *Ethics: The Essential Writings*, edited by Gordon Daniel Marino, 506–529. New York: Modern Library, 2010.

Marino, Gordon Daniel. "A Sand County Almanac." In *Ethics: The Essential Writings*, edited by Gordon Daniel Marino, 486–505. New York: Modern Library, 2010.

Mogi, Ken. *Awakening Your Ikigai: How the Japanese Wake up to Joy and Purpose Every Day*. Ntw York: The Experiment, 2018.

Newport, Cal. *Deep Work: Rules for Focused Success in a Distracted World*. New York: Grand Central Publishing, 2018.

Plato. *The Apology*. Edited by Benjamin Jowett. Sioux Falls, SD: Nuvision Publications, 2004.

Plato. *Republic*. Translated by Christopher Emlyn-Jones and William Preddy. Cambridge, MA: Harvard University Press, 2013.

Sartre, Jean-Paul. *No Exit and Three Other Plays*. Translated by Stuart Gilbert, edited by Lionel Abel. Leesburg, VA: Paw Prints, 2008.

Snodgrass, Mary Ellen. *The Metamorphosis: Franz Kafka*. Chicago, IL: Perma-Bound, 1989.

Thoreau, Henry David. *Walking*. Edited by Adam-Max Tuchinsky. Thomaston, ME: Tilbury House Publishers, 2017.

WORKS CITED

Antoninus, Marcus Aurelius, and John Jackson. *The Thoughts of Marcus Aurelius Antoninus*. London: Oxford University Press, 1962.

Aristotle. *Nicomachean Ethics*. In *Ethics: The Essential Writings*, edited by Gordon Daniel Marino, 43–84. New York: Modern Library, 2010.

Aristotle. In *A Presocratics Reader: Selected Fragments and Testimonia*, edited by Patricia Curd. Indianapolis, IN: Hackett Publishing, 2011.

Beauvoir, Simone de. *The Coming of Age*. Edited by Patrick O'Brian. New York: Norton, 1996.

Beauvoir, Simone de. *The Book of Positive Quotations*. Edited by John Cook, Steve Deger, and Leslie Ann Gibson, 548. Minneapolis, MN: Fairview Press, 2007.

Camus, Albert. *The Myth of Sisyphus, and Other Essays*. Translated by Justin O'Brien. New York: Vintage Books, 1961.

Camus, Albert. *The Plague*. Translated by Stuart Gilbert. New York: Vintage Books, 1991.

Chödrön, Pema. *The Pocket Pema Chödrön*. Edited by Eden Steinberg. Boulder, CO: Shambhala, 2017.

Cicero, Marcus Tullius., and Michael Grant. *Cicero: Selected Works*. Harmondsworth, England: Penguin Books, 1965.

Confucius. *The Analects*. Translated by Raymond Dawson. New York: Oxford University Press, 2003.

Dewey, John. *Democracy and Education*. Radford, VA: Wilder Publications, 2008.

Dostoyevsky, Fyodor. *The Idiot*. Harmondsworth, UK: Penguin Books, 1961.

Dostoyevsky, Fyodor. *Notes from Underground.* Translated by Richard Pevear and Larissa Volokhonsky. New York: Alfred A. Knopf, 1993.

Epictetus. *The Art of Living: The Classic Manual on Virtue, Happiness, and Effectiveness.* Edited by Sharon Lebell. New York: HarperOne, 2007.

Epictetus. *The Enchiridion.* Cambridge, MA: Classics.MIT. Accessed April 08, 2018. http://classics.mit.edu/Epictetus/epicench.html.

Al-Fārābi. Directing Attention to the Way to Happiness. In *Classical Arabic Philosophy: An Anthology of Sources,* edited by John McGinnis and David C. Reisman, 104–120. Indianapolis, IN: Hackett Publishing Company, 2007.

Friedmann, Georges. *La Puissance et la Sagesse.* Paris: Gallimard, 1970.

Hadot, Pierre. *Philosophy as a Way of Life: Spiritual Exercises from Socrates to Foucault.* Edited by Arnold Ira Davidson. Oxford: Blackwell, 1995.

Heraclitus. In *A Presocratics Reader: Selected Fragments and Testimonia.* Edited by Patricia Curd. Indianapolis, IN: Hackett Publishing, 2011.

Hsun Tzu. *Basic Writings.* Edited by Burton Watson. New York: Columbia University Press, 1997.

James, William. *The Will to Believe: And Other Essays in Popular Philosophy, and Human Immortality.* Mineola, NY: Dover Publications, 2015.

Kierkegaard, Søren. *The Sickness Unto Death: Part II.* In *Ethics: The Essential Writings,* edited by Gordon Daniel Marino, 299–305. New York: Modern Library, 2010.

Al-Kindī. *On the Means of Dispelling Sorrows.* In *Classical Arabic Philosophy: An Anthology of Sources,* edited by John McGinnis and David C. Reisman, 23–35. Indianapolis, IN: Hackett Publishing Company, 2007.

King, Martin Luther. *A Gift of Love: Sermons from Strength to Love and Other Preachings*. Edited by Raphael G. Warnock and Coretta Scott King. London: Penguin, 2017.

Lao Tzu. *Chinese Classics: Tao Te Ching*. Edited by Dim C. Lau. Harmondsworth, UK: Penguin Books, 1964.

Marcus Aurelius. *Meditations*. Edited by George Long. Seattle, WA: CreateSpace Independent Publishing Platform, 2017.

Mill, John Stuart. *Utilitarianism*. In *Ethics: The Essential Writings*, edited by Gordon Daniel Marino, 225–255. New York: Modern Library, 2010.

Nhat Hanh, Thich. *How to Love*. London: Rider, 2016.

Nhat Hanh, Thich. *How to Walk*. Berkeley, CA: Parallax Pr, 2016.

Ortega y Gasset, José. *Man and Crisis*. Edited by Mildred Adams. New York: Norton & Company, 1962.

Plato. *Crito*. In *Ethics: The Essential Writings*, edited by Gordon Daniel Marino, 24–37. New York: Modern Library, 2010.

Plato. *Republic*. Translated by Christopher Emlyn-Jones and William Preddy. Cambridge, MA: Harvard University Press, 2013.

Plotinus. *The Enneads: A New, Definitive Edition with Comparisons to Other Translations on Hundreds of Key Passages*. Translated by Stephen Mackenna. Burdett, NY: Published for the Paul Brunton Philosophic Foundation by Larson Publications, 1992.

Ar-Rāzī. *The Philosopher's Way of Life*. In *Classical Arabic Philosophy: An Anthology of Sources*, edited by John McGinnis and David C. Reisman, 36–44. Indianapolis, IN: Hackett Publishing Company, 2007.

Sartre, Jean-Paul. *Existentialism is a Humanism: Including, A Commentary on the Stranger*. Edited by Arlette Elkaïm-Sartre, translated by Carol Macomber. New Haven, CT: Yale University Press, 2007.

Seneca, Lucius Annaeus. *Seneca Six Pack: Six Essential Texts.* Translated by Richard M. Gummere, Ella Isabel Harris, Aubrey Stewart. Los Angeles, CA: Enhanced Media Publishing, 2016.

Sun Tzu. *Art of War*. Minneapolis, MN: Filiquarian Publishing, 2012.

Tolstoy, Leo. *Essays, Letters, Miscellanies.* New York: Scribner, 1929

West, Cornel. Cit. in Kristen Olson. *Wounded by School: Recapturing the Joy in Learning and Standing up to Old School Culture.* New York: Teachers College Press, 2009.